SUCCESSFUL
INTERVIEW
SKILLS

SUCCESSFUL
INTERVIEW
SKILLS

HOW TO PRESENT
YOURSELF WITH
CONFIDENCE

SECOND EDITION

REBECCA CORFIELD

KOGAN
PAGE

To TB

First published in 1992, reprinted 1995, 1996 (twice), 1997, 1998
Second edition 1999, reprinted 2000 (twice)

Kogan Page Limited
120 Pentonville Road
London N1 9JN

© Rebecca Corfield, 1992, 1999

British Library Cataloguing in Publication Data

A CIP record for this book is available from the British Library.

ISBN 0 7494 2978 X

Typeset by Saxon Graphics Ltd, Derby
Printed and bound by Clays Ltd, St Ives plc

Contents

Contents

Introduction

The importance of interviews

Interviews are a fact of modern life and interview skills will be used by us all many times throughout our lives. Most jobs are filled as a result of one-to-one meetings between the employer and the best candidates, but interview skills are needed in a variety of situations. Whether applying for a job, a promotion, a training programme, a college course, or even a bank loan, we all need to know about the processes involved in the interview and how to impress other people at first meeting. With part time and temporary work increasing, we will all be attending interviews more frequently in the future.

The skills involved in creating a favourable impression on others and presenting ourselves to them at interview are the same skills that make us confident at meeting people in any situation – whether at work or socially.

Interviews are difficult at the best of times. Whether applying for a job or a course, appearing before just one person or a panel, you need to know how to present yourself confidently and enthusiastically. Interviews are often seen as the major hurdle between us and the job we want. But an interview, whether for a job vacancy or anything else, is a marvellous opportunity. Why? Because you are in control of most of the impressions that the interviewer has of you.

You, for instance, will decide how to dress and act, and exactly what you want to convey about yourself. No one else can *make* you look or behave in a way that you do not want to. In the same way you cannot be made to say anything you do not agree with. You must admit that this is a comforting thought. Although it may be difficult to believe, the interview will mostly go the way that you want it to. Of course, you will not be in control of the selection of the interview panel or the other candidates, but there are many things you can do to improve your chances of appearing as the best person for the job.

Many people think that it is a pure fluke whether they are successful in interviews or not. To them the outcome seems to depend on whether the face fits, being in the right place at the right time or some other unidentifiable cause. But the outcome of the interview process is *not* determined by chance. We can exercise considerable control and influence over the way the interview is conducted and, more important, over the outcome.

How to get the most out of this book

This book can show you how to exercise more control over interviews. Whether you are applying for jobs at the moment, learning about interview techniques for the first time, advising other people on the best way to approach interviews, or just want to refresh your techniques for the future, this book will be able to help. For no matter how many times you face the interviewer across the table, you can still learn how to refine and improve your performance and put yourself across more positively.

Some of the advice given may seem to be common sense but, when running training courses in interviewing skills and personal presentation, I am often surprised that such basic skills need re-stating, and that is why they are included here.

Of course, I do not claim that this book will make you successful at getting *any* job, and I assume that you will only be applying for those vacancies for which you can reasonably expect to be considered. However, if we study the candidates who are successful at interview, we will discover some common characteristics.

Chapter 1 describes the different kinds of interview and explains what happens in an interview. Looking specifically at job interviews, we consider what the employer is trying to achieve at an interview. A typical interview is described and the different stages of preparing for an interview are outlined. Chapter 2 looks at the whole process from the employer's point of view and shows the importance of planning and preparation. Chapter 3 offers suggestions about what to say in interviews and explains how to analyse what the employer is looking for.

Chapter 4 examines other aspects of presentation and looks at what contributes to the impression we make on other people. Body language, controlling nerves and personal image are all covered. Chapter 5 gives sample questions and suggested answers, covers how to handle tricky situations, and provides a handy list of 'dos and don'ts' for your next interview. The concluding chapter draws together all the information and gives you a step-by-step guide to successful interview skills.

CHAPTER 1

The interview process

What is an interview?

The dictionary defines an interview as a face-to-face meeting for the purposes of consultation. In other words, it is a discussion for one reason or another.

By far the biggest cost to an employer is the staff or workforce. Wages and salaries often make up 70 per cent of a business's total costs, and the cost of advertising for staff is high. Obviously decisions about who to employ have to be taken seriously.

It is therefore not surprising that employers spend a great deal of time and money trying to ensure that they pick the right person for each job. In this context, the right person means the individual who will contribute most to the good of the company or organisation and who will repay the time and money spent on him or her as an employee by staying with the company and performing well.

People who interview you for a job are likely to be complete strangers. Interviews normally take place sitting down and can range from an informal chat in easy chairs over a coffee table to a formal panel interview (ie with more than one person interviewing) across a leather-topped desk. Interviews for jobs with larger companies are sometimes part of a much more complicated selection procedure which can involve exercises, group activities and tests.

Sometimes these selection procedures take place at what is called an assessment centre, often based at the head office of the organisation concerned. You may also be asked to give a presentation on some aspect of the position applied for, as part of the selection process. If this is the case it will be made clear in your letter of introduction to the interview.

Interviews come in many shapes and sizes. Not all interviews are to do with applying for jobs. You may be interviewed for a place at college or on a training course, for voluntary work or to join a club or society. Many of us will frequently be interviewed when we are in a job or studying, by our supervisors, managers or tutors to appraise our progress, help with our development or sort out work or study problems.

Why do interviews take place?

Interviews are held to gather information. In an interview for a job the employer is interested in finding out which of the short-listed candidates (those chosen for interview) would be the most suitable person for the job.

If I asked you to find out about somebody whom you had never met before, you would probably choose to talk to that person face to face. Interviews are just a common-sense way for people to find out about each other and ask each other questions. So, as well as the employer seeing you, you also have the chance to make your own decisions about the employer, the job on offer and the type of organisation or company concerned.

What happens in an interview?

After applying for a job, you will be informed that the employer wishes you to attend at a specific place and time and you will probably be one of a group of people who have been short-listed or chosen, from all the others who also applied for the position, to be seen individually by the employer.

When you arrive at the company, if you have not already completed an application form, you may be asked to complete a form giving your personal details. At the appointed time you will be called in to the interview room and invited to sit facing your interviewer, often across a table or desk.

The employer will ask you questions for a period of between 20 minutes and an hour on average, depending on the type of job applied for and the level of your experience and qualifications. At the end of this time you may be able to ask the employer some questions relating to the position applied for. (Chapter 3 contains more information about the type of questions that you may want to ask at this point.) This normally marks the end of the interview.

It is quite common for the interviewer to take notes about your answers in order to remember the main points after your discussion. For some jobs you will be asked to prepare a presentation on your ideas for the position. If so, this usually takes place before your interview begins. It can be a valuable chance to put across ideas you think can contribute to the organisation.

What are interviews about?

Interviews are like examinations at the end of a course. You know that you have done well so far on the course, and you know in advance roughly what areas the questions are going to cover. In the same way you know that you have done well in the selection process up to this point, or the employer would not have invited you for the interview. You also know in advance roughly what will be covered in the questions to be asked because you have studied the details relating to the job, and you have read this book!

What leads to success in interviews?

In the same way as thorough preparation leads to success in examinations, so a system for approaching interviews can have the same outcome. Most of the talking done in the interview will be by you. This means that you have a fair measure of control in deciding where the interview is going. Of course, you cannot set all the questions yourself, but you can calculate fairly accurately what subject areas will be covered and plan your answers accordingly.

Even the most successful careerist will fail many interviews, but still end up in rewarding and challenging work. The best approach is to try to present yourself in the best way and treat each interview as a learning experience.

CHAPTER 2

What employers are looking for

The only reason why you will be invited to an interview is because the employer wants to find out more about you to ascertain whether you are the best candidate for the job. Sometimes people believe that they are called in to be tested with trick questions or put under pressure. This is very rarely the case. No sensible employer can afford the time for, or the expense of, such games. You will be interviewed for one purpose only – to find out exactly who you are and how you would deal with certain situations likely to crop up in the job.

You are only there because your initial approach, whether through application form or curriculum vitae (CV), has interested the employer enough to want to know more. Whatever you have said so far has worked.

How to provide proof that you are the right candidate

If you have been called for an interview, there is no reason why you should not get the job. To capitalise on your success so far, you must research thoroughly exactly what you put in your CV or application. Let us consider the interview for a moment. What is happening there? A strange relationship has been set up – we do not normally have to talk to total strangers about our background, experiences and personality in such a one-sided way.

The situation arises because the employer has something that we want – the job – and we are 'on show' to convince him

What the employer is looking for

or her that we are the most suitable candidate for that particular job. Now the most suitable candidate may not necessarily be the best in terms of either experience or skills, but will be the person who seems to fit in best and is most impressive at the interview.

Employers are interested in three main areas:

- your qualifications and skills;

- your experience and work background;

- your personality and what sort of person you are.

The most important of these is the last one. I have known candidates who fall short of the advertised skills and qualifications for a job, and often lack the requisite experience, but who still manage to convince the employer that they are the best candidates on offer. How? By stressing that they have the right personality to fit into the organisation and contribute fully to the fortunes of that company. Skills can be taught and experience gained on the job, if necessary – but you cannot change your personality so easily.

In my research with employers, these are the most common reasons for failure at interview.

- Not answering the question fully or properly, eg too short answers or just lots of waffle.

- Not showing any excitement or enthusiasm for the work.

- Not being clear about their skills and abilities, eg being too vague or too modest.

- Using pretentious language or jargon instead of normal speech.

- Not showing that they have fully considered all aspects of the vacancy, eg indicating a dislike of paperwork when it is obvious that it is a large part of the job on offer.

Reasons for success

Qualities in demand by most employers include being flexible; having a caring and helpful attitude to clients, customers and colleagues; enjoying working in a team; showing keenness to take on responsibility for organising people or projects; being positive in your attitude in the face of difficulties or changes and displaying enthusiasm for the work. Evidence of continual learning is impressive, as is evidence of being able to handle change.

De-mystifying the interview

Employers are often bad at interviewing people. Have you ever had an interview where the employer did all the talking, or where he or she just did not manage to put you at ease at all, or where he or she arrived late and seemed confused about the exact job applied for? This sort of thing can happen when the interviewer is either not competent, not trained or not prepared for the occasion. Many people who are roped in to conduct interviews have had little or no formal training in this subject. Even if they have, it takes the right kind of personality to be good at interviewing other people and bring out interviewees' good points.

However, defects in the interviewers' technique need not matter too much, although it can be helpful to be forewarned about such a possibility. Ultimately, it is up to you to prepare yourself so well that the interviewer's shortcomings will not distract you from putting your skills, experience and personality over positively. **You need to convince the employer that you have a lot to offer the company.** Think about this from the employer's point of view.

Stressing your contribution

Imagine that you run a company and need to employ an administrator. You already know that *everyone* who applies wants the job, and that it would improve their career prospects should they be successful. You do not necessarily

want to hear at the interview how beneficial it would be for the candidates to get the job, because all the applicants will feel the same way.

As the employer you want to hear what the candidates are going to offer *you* and what they can contribute to your organisation. The days have long gone when employers had difficulty in attracting applicants for vacancies. Now, assuming that you have advertised appropriately, you will have a good selection of people applying for your vacancy. The main question that you want answered is: 'Which one of the people I am interviewing today would offer most as an employee?'

Remember:

1. If you have been called for an interview, there is no reason why you should not get the job.
2. The most important factor to convey is that you are the right sort of person for the job.
3. Employers are often bad at interviewing people.
4. You need to convince the employer that you have a lot to offer.

Importance of planning and preparation

Imagine that you have applied for a job you very much want. Today, 'plop' on to the doormat, comes a letter inviting you for an interview. Congratulations! So far everything you have done has impressed the employer. Now that we have more of an idea of the principles behind the interviewing process, we can look in more detail at what to say. PLANNING and PREPARATION give you CONFIDENCE which leads to ENTHUSIASM and SUCCESS.

Planning
First comes the planning stage. You are ready to work out what you need to say in the interview. Let us examine the

heart of the question – how can you know what you should say in the interview? As indicated earlier, the interview is like an examination where you have been told the main subject areas for questioning in advance. The source of your information comes from what you have already been told or have found out about the job on offer.

CHAPTER 3
What to say in interviews

Setting up a system

The first stage of planning is to collect all the information you can about the vacancy and the organisation. You will rarely be invited for interview without being given some clues as to the sort of candidate required. If the job was advertised and you have been sent a job description or, even better, a person specification, you have as good as been told all the answers.

A job description, as the name suggests, details the main duties of the job and a person specification explains what sort of person the employer is looking for. Both these documents are very useful. Make sure you pay careful attention to all the documents that you receive about the job. The employer will have gone to a lot of time and trouble to write down what the post involves. You will be expected to show evidence that you have a lot to offer for each and every part of it.

Selling yourself

In the past when applicants for positions were much fewer, carefully working through these documents to show that you had the necessary experience and character would have been enough to get you an interview. Nowadays, with so much more competition, it is not just a question of paying attention to detail but of finding ways to 'sell yourself'. Such an expression seems to apply more to washing powder than to human beings, but it is a good term to use.

Consider an advertisement for Sudso washing powder on the television. We are not just shown a box of Sudso and told to buy it. We may be shown a washing line full of sparkling white clothes to demonstrate exactly what the product can do. We are told repeatedly that it washes whiter; gives our clothes a lovely, fresh smell; is substantially cheaper than its rivals; comes in a refillable pack; removes dirt and stains, etc.

Because of all the other advertisements for similar products, the message is hammered home. But when we watch an advert like this, it does not seem as though the message has been too strong; rather, we are left with the impression that it may be a product we ought to try. This is the effect we want to create with the interviewer by using the invited time available to promote our strengths and positive attributes.

Analysing the job

The job description

By looking closely at the details in the job description you can see what the employer expects the job-holder to do. The tasks are sometimes split up into those where some experience is essential and others where experience is preferred. Ideally, you need to go through the following steps:

- Work through the job description.

- Underline or mark the words which mention the main activities of the job (the verbs).

- Make rough notes to show how you have gained experience of all these activities – think of an example from your background or work experience.

- Convert your rough notes into a written or typed form that gives answers to questions on each of the points that you have underlined.

- Revisit the information that you provided on your application form, adding more and different examples as appropriate.

The person specification

This document is often sent out for vacancies in large companies, local authorities or the civil service, all of which have large personnel departments. It contains useful information about the type of person the organisation is looking for. Your approach to this information should be the same as for the job description.

- Study it carefully to see what characteristics are either *essential* for the job or *preferred* and underline both.

- Work through each of these items in rough, noting down an example from your own background which shows how your personality fits closely with what is required. You must provide proof that you have all the characteristics marked as essential to be successful in the interview.

- Write your answers in proper sentences so that you can rehearse them for the actual interview.

- If you completed an application form for this job previously, retrace your steps to fully prepare your answers on how you meet the person specification.

How to find out more

You may want to contact the company either formally or informally to find out more about their operations. By a formal contact I mean telephoning and talking to the person in charge of personnel or the local manager. For example:

'I have been invited for an interview with your company/organisation soon and I wondered if there was any more information available about your products/services.'

There may be a specific question that you want answered, such as:

'Are all your offices based around London?'

Some people are happier not revealing that they are coming for an interview and say that they are doing research and want some information. Public companies publish annual reports which contain useful background on the major recent projects undertaken.

Companies often advertise their products or services in magazines, local and national newspapers, and on the World Wide Web. These advertisements can show you how the company presents itself, and tell you which are its main products.

Thinking about the job

When you are satisfied that you have gathered as much material as possible in the time available, you need to start thinking hard about the likely subjects to be covered at interview. To start with, though, consider the following advertisement, seen in a local paper:

STOCK HANDLER

Busy high street store requires seasonal stock handlers to work in their warehouse, sorting and checking stock. Training given but experience useful.

Now what can we tell, from this short advertisement, about the person required? Even without a job description or a person specification, and without knowing the name of the company, we can use our common sense to deduce the following. The person will need to be fit and healthy in order to carry boxes of stock around. There is bound to be a certain amount of paperwork and administration, involving completing and checking stock record cards, so the right candidate will need to be literate and numerate. Computer experience, or at least a willingness to learn, might be useful.

The store is likely to be a large one if it has its own warehouse, so the work will probably involve working with teams of people. Someone with a friendly and flexible approach is needed. Accuracy will be important and care will have to be taken with the stock because of the value of the goods handled. The candidate should be honest and able to be trusted with valuables.

All these duties and characteristics can be inferred from the brief details given in the advert. We could get much more of an idea of the person required if we had been given a job description and a person specification. But even without them, there is no excuse for not thinking through what the employer is looking for as part of your preparation.

If you are not prepared to do some planning before the event, and do not feel that you can get excited about the vacancy, it may mean that you are not serious about applying for the position. Generally, if a job is worth going for, it is worth spending time preparing for, and that involves sifting through all the infor-mation at your disposal for clues about the successful candidate.

Giving a presentation

Sometimes you will be asked to give a short presentation as part of the interview. This will not be sprung on you. The employer will have explained what is required when you were invited for the session. If the letter sent does not make it completely clear what you have to do, do not hesitate to ring up and ask for more information.

Presentations are normally only requested if public speak-ing is central to the position applied for, eg public relations assistant, training officer, marketing executive. They are a way of giving you a block of time in which to make your case in whichever way you like. This means that you have the chance to provide extra information about why you think you would be the best person for the job.

Types of presentation

Here are some examples of different presentations that could be requested:

- Please prepare a five-minute presentation on your ideas for this position.

- Please come with a fifteen-minute outline of your priorities in this role.

- We would like you to talk for ten minutes about the key issues you think are facing this organisation.
- Please have ready a ten-minute outline of your main work achievements to date.

- We would like you to talk for five minutes on why we should give you this job.

Often you will be offered an overhead projector, flip chart or other visual aids to use if they would be a normal part of the job. Do not try and use anything that you are not confident and comfortable with. When under stress is not the best time to experiment with unknown bits of machinery.

Preparing a presentation

With a speech to present you need to prepare even more fully. Try and structure your session into three key points so that it is easy to follow. Do not try and pack too much information in, as a few clear points are better than a lot of confused material. Practise what you want to say in front of:

- a mirror, so that you know how you are going to look;
- friends, so that you can check that what you are saying makes sense;
- the clock, so that you can time your presentation accurately.

Remember that the impression you want the employer to retain is that you are the person with the most to offer because of your appropriate background (skills and experience), your personality and your good ideas for the role.

Areas of likely questioning

It was stated earlier that an employer will be interested in three main areas of questioning. You know without a doubt that you will be asked questions about (a) your qualifications and skills; (b) your previous work experience; and (c) your character or personality. Let us look at each of these areas in turn.

(a) Your qualifications and skills

Before you are interviewed it is helpful to have prepared a good CV. This document is useful for interviews as well as job applications as it should contain a concise list of courses taken and jobs held. Before the interview you will need to make a thorough review of your background, especially if you have taken several different courses. Fluffing your answers when you are unsure of your ground is all too apparent to an interviewer and looks unprofessional.

You will then be completely familiar with what you have spent time studying, and where and when. You almost need to be able to recite your CV in your sleep! As a result, when you are asked questions about your educational background, the information you require will come easily and concisely.

When you are being interviewed and are asked about your past studies, the employer does not want to hear you recite a list of the courses you have attended. Think *why* the employer should be interested in such information. The reason is that he or she wants to know *what you learned* from your studies. In most cases, therefore, it is more important to get across the main subjects studied, what projects you specifically worked on, which exams you passed – if any – and which parts of the course you enjoyed most, or learned most from.

Those who have not taken any exams will still be expected to talk about courses studied at school or college. You will need to work out which were your favourite subjects, which lessons you felt benefited you most, and why.

(b) Your previous work experience

The same is true of your work experience. All your jobs and the details of what you did as your main duties need to be at the front of your mind. You should not assume that it is obvious to an interviewer what you did as a filing clerk. Most interviewers will be interested in the precise skills used in the job that could help you to contribute to the position applied for.

You may think that all filing clerks file – but what sort of documents were you dealing with? Were they important legal papers or plans, originals of letters or clients' personal details? Perhaps you used to file things by number rather than alphabetically, or you might have had to cross-reference materials. Did you ever have to retrieve records in a hurry, work under pressure or trace missing papers? Did you ever use particular computer packages, answer queries from the public or liaise with colleagues from other departments?

All these things could be what are called *transferable skills,* ie skills that you learn or use in one job which can be transferred to the next. The advantage to an employer should be obvious. Your skill in one area of work, in which you can demonstrate expertise, means that you will not need training to do the same thing in the next job.

Again, let us consider *why* the interviewer is asking this type of question. The answer is, to see what kind of an employee you would make. Therefore, *when* you worked in a particular place is not as important as *what you contributed there,* since it gives the employer an idea of your capabilities.

(c) Your character or personality

Of the three main areas of interest to an employer, the greatest importance attaches to the type of person you are. It happens again and again; even if a candidate's educational background or previous experience is not up to those of his or her competitors, by demonstrating certain advantages involving personality or character, the candidate is successful in getting the job. Why should this be so? As long as a candidate is the sort of person who will fit into the company and who enjoys his or her work, that person can easily be trained to compensate for any lack of skills or experience.

Sharing the vision
There is one further aspect for employers to consider when they are interviewing. Many candidates may seem to have appropriate qualifications, experience and personality to fit the vacancy. What else could make the difference between the best and the rest? If candidates can show that they have thought about the job, specifically the contribution that they can make and the way that the job should be done, they cannot fail but impress.

This requires spending some time thinking about the key aspects of the job. What are the strengths and weaknesses of the organisation as far as you can tell? What can you discover about the environment in which the company is operating? Think about both the job and the organisation and try and analyse which factors might be important.

For instance, if the vacancy is with a commercial company, who are its competitors? What is your image of the product or service provided? Are there any changes taking place in the wider world that might affect the company's business? What about the nature of the specific job concerned? What do you see as the most important features of the job and why? How do you imagine yourself doing the job and what special contribution would you make?

Spending time developing your ideas or vision about the future for the organisation shows both your commitment and interest in the job and the likely added value that you could bring compared to other candidates. Most employers do not have the time to think about the specific details of every job in their organisation. They want to recruit people who can do the job well on their behalf and bring in fresh ideas and energy to the task. You will enhance the impression you make if you can also talk intelligently about your vision of the organisation and your role in it.

Mind the gap! Covering up your weak spots

We all have something we would prefer the interviewer didn't linger over. For some it may be time spent unemployed; for others it may be something in their past that they would prefer to cover up, such as a lot of job changes or having stayed too long in a dead-end job. Few people have a perfect career history, owing to various circumstances, eg having a family, a period of ill-health, previous or current unemployment, imprisonment or detention.

What is important is that you think through and practise how to deal with these gaps. It means learning, not how to lie, but how to put forward positively a cogent and convincing explanation of the relevant experience you have gained in the past.

Maximising your strengths

Another approach is not to cover up past experiences but to present them in a different way. This requires you to make a virtue out of things that happened to you through necessity. Let us look at an example. Imagine someone who has had several different jobs in a short space of time. The best way to justify this is to work out how this will concern an employer. So let us climb inside the mind of an employer who is faced with an interviewee called Deborah.

Deborah has had six jobs in the last five years and is applying to join W Sayer's company as a personal assistant. Mr Sayer, the managing director, is concerned that Deborah may want to leave this job in a few months' time. If that happened he would have to repeat the expensive and time-consuming task of selecting another employee. He is worried too that she will not settle into the position, that she will not take the work seriously and that she will not show enough commitment to the company.

Deborah realises that these job changes are something she should present positively to the interviewer. She does not imply that she was unhappy in any of her previous jobs but suggests that, even if she did not stay long in any one position, the employers were glad to have her even for a limited time because of the contribution she was able to make.

She spends time before the interview thinking about what she contributed in each of her previous jobs and what it was that made her want to move each time. In other words, she worked out her story in advance and planned what information she wanted to convey in the interview.

Learning from experience

Whenever you attend an interview make a note immediately afterwards of the questions you were asked and how you replied. Evaluate what happened. Did any of the questions take you by surprise? If so, they need fuller preparation next time. Which of your answers seemed to go down well? Why was that? Continuous improvement comes from looking back and learning in this way.

Golden rules

1. Always be positive about previous jobs

It is important always to be positive about *every* job that you have had in the past. Why should this be so vital? Again, let us consider it from the employer's point of view. Will it impress an interviewer to hear a candidate saying what a bad boss his or her last employer was? Will it sound good to hear another company being put down or maligned by a candidate, or will it make the employer think that the candidate could well be saying the same sort of thing about this company in a few years' time?

Someone who moans about other organisations also creates an impression of surliness and a negative attitude. Nobody will be interested in employing such a candidate. The positive and keen candidate will be preferred.

2. Be enthusiastic and keen

Nothing attracts people like enthusiasm. The candidate who exhibits such a characteristic has a great advantage, almost before anything else is said or taken into consideration. We are all more interested in working with the person who comes into work each day in a good mood and feeling positive about the job, rather than with the moaner or trouble-maker who is always being negative.

3. Capitalise on your strengths

The only things that the interviewer knows about you are what you have put in your application or CV and what you are going to talk about in the actual interview. Therefore, what you say about yourself dictates the impression that the interviewer will have of you, ie your skills, experience and personality. The interviewer will be looking at you as a potential worker or member of staff – you need to imply that everything you have been doing so far has been leading up to this job, with this organisation, at this time. Couple that with your vision of the way the job should be handled from now on. Irresistible!

Which questions to ask?

At the end of the interview, you will usually be asked if you have any questions to put. Do not feel obliged to ask something just for the sake of it. Only ask a question if it is necessary. If you feel that you know all you need to about the job on offer, it is fine to say something like:

'I think that you have covered all the important points already, thank you. But if I have any questions later I will contact you.'

Do not ask questions about uniforms, holidays or other practical points. If you are offered the post you will be informed about this kind of detail when you start.

If pay has not been mentioned so far, this is not the time to raise the issue. You would probably not accept any position without knowing the wages, but again you can find this out once you receive the offer of the job, when you could reply:

'I am interested in the job at this stage, but I am still not quite sure about the conditions of employment. Can you tell me exactly what the wages and hours are?'

If you do decide to ask the interviewer some questions, it is a good idea to show your general attitude in the type of thing you say. Questions about training opportunities or the chance to take on greater responsibilities in the future show that you are keen, plan to stay in the job, and are interested in moving up the organisation.

CHAPTER 4

Presenting yourself

The importance of presentation

You may be asking why a chapter in a book on interviewing skills should be about presenting yourself. Surely the most important thing to learn is what to say in the interview? On the contrary, the impression we make on other people consists of much more than just the words we speak. A large part of the way we judge other people comes from first impressions. In other words, what we notice in the first quick glance, which may last for only 30 seconds, is the way they look and behave.

In fact, research has shown that 55 per cent of this first impression is based on appearance and behaviour, which can include clothing, posture, body language and facial expressions. Thirty-eight per cent of the impression is from the way we speak, which includes the way the voice is used, clarity of speech and accent. Only 7 per cent is from the words we say.

Just consider this startling information for a moment. It means that a whole 93 per cent of that all-important first impression we make on other people is rooted in *what we look like and the way we sound*. However, this is not information to be depressed about; on the contrary, it gives us much more control over the extent to which we can impress other people, especially interviewers.

Creating a positive first impression

If you are now saying that you personally do not judge others by such superficial measures, consider these percentages when you next meet people for the first time. Imagine you are at a party and want to make some new friends. Looking round the room, you notice someone whom you have not met before. She looks a bit dowdy and is standing alone with a worried expression on her face. She is looking at the floor with her shoulders slightly hunched and, although someone is trying to talk to her, she does not seem to be contributing much to the conversation.

Now you notice somebody else. She is smartly dressed, has a twinkle in her eye and is chatting animatedly to someone. She has just grinned at you in a friendly way, and you notice that she is standing up tall and looking confident. Which one of these two people would you be most likely to talk to?

Even though we may not like the fact that we are being judged by others on their first impression of us, we are doing exactly the same to other people all the time. We all have prejudices about what we like to look at and what sort of behaviour we think is appropriate at different times. The secret of success is in understanding how other people perceive you and using this information to your advantage. Interviewers will make many allowances for a well-presented candidate.

The information in this chapter will be useful in many situations – not just at interviews. Once you know how to create a good first impression, you can be the person at the party whom everyone wants to meet! But creating a good first impression at an interview is doubly important because so much is at stake when you meet potential employers.

It is your responsibility to make sure that the impression you create works in your favour. This does not mean trying to put on an act or pretending to be someone else, as this is obvious to the interviewer; rather, you want to enhance your strong points and minimise your weaker ones.

It was stated that 55 per cent of first impressions are created by the way we look and behave, 38 per cent by the way we sound and only 7 per cent by what we say. Let us look at each of these areas in turn.

Appearance

Your appearance is the most important aspect of the first impression you create. This cannot be stressed too much, and if it is the only thing you learn from reading this book, it will be valuable. The advice in this section applies equally to men and women. A smart appearance shows that you have taken trouble over the way you look. A plain neutral appearance indicates a serious, professional outlook. Your choice of clothes indicates your attitude to yourself and other people.

Women will be more familiar with the points made because they tend to be exposed to more advice and information about appearance than men, but this generally leads merely to lack of confidence. Being bombarded with messages about fashion and advertisements from the clothing and cosmetics industries only serves to worry women. It is similar to being spoilt for choice in a larger supermarket compared to the relatively simple choices of a corner shop – the shopping experience in the supermarket can lead to confusion. Interviews are difficult enough without adding the burden of concern about our appearance. The aim here is to eradicate this particular anxiety.

You do not want to appear showy or quirky in your choice of clothes but you should look clean and smart. I am often asked whether it is possible to be overdressed for an interview. I do not think so (with the possible exception of a dinner jacket or ball gown!). Even if the job would normally require you to wear overalls or a uniform, dressing with care for your interview shows you have taken time over your appearance and indicates an awareness of being, to some extent, on show.

Men should wear a dark suit, or at least a smart jacket and tie for a job where less formal clothing is the norm. Women should dress smartly (a jacket is a good idea), and not be cluttered with accessories. Whatever the job, it is good when you are feeling nervous to add authority to the impression you create.

Colour and style of clothes

It is generally acknowledged that there is a particular range of colours that suits an individual best. These colours will be different for everybody but can help to give each of us a distinct presence. The right clothes do not draw attention to themselves; rather, they show off the person inside them, and in the right colours you will receive compliments on how well you are looking rather than on your clothes.

As a rule, plain neutral colours are safest when you want to look smart. Navy blue or medium to dark grey for suits or jackets and a soft white or ivory shirt or blouse work well for a confident, competent appearance.

Don't confuse looking attractive or pretty with looking business-like. Keep your clothes for getting attention for your social life and let your abilities and ideas do the talking in the interview.

Image consultants give professional advice on the colour and style of clothes to suit your natural colouring and body shape. The advice given is based on the idea of tailoring the colours you wear to those in your natural colouring. The same applies to the style of your clothes. You have a certain body shape which can be echoed in your clothes to show you to your best advantage. This applies to a greater extent to women because of the more extensive range of styles and colours available to them, but it is also relevant to men – in particular to the shape and style of their clothes.

An initial consultation with an image consultant does not cost the earth. The money spent on one session of colour and style analysis with a good image consultant is easily compensated for by the time and money you will save when you no longer make 'shopping mistakes'. If you go to a professional for advice on your health, hair, teeth, psychological problems, pets, etc why not go to a professional for advice on the most important part of your image? You will be advised which clothes make you look your best, what you will be most comfortable in, and what is most appropriate for different occasions. Look in the telephone directory for consultants in your area.

Be aware of your appearance from every angle. I once knew a candidate who forgot to do this and only realised after the interview that her scarlet petticoat was visible under her smart black interview skirt.

Accessories
Ties, shoes, belts, bags and jewellery can make or break an outfit, although we think of them as additions to our general look. Shoes are often noticed and should be clean and smart for an interview. Dangling earrings should be left for evening wear, as should jingly bracelets. Jewellery is not generally considered acceptable on men and so remove it for the duration of the interview. Men should wear calf-length socks that stay up, in the same colours as their shoes. Women should carry only one bag. If you take a briefcase, put your handbag items in it. Don't juggle with both a briefcase and a handbag.

Hair
Your hair should be clean and recently cut. If you have an important interview approaching, visit a good hairdresser and ask for advice on the best style for you. If you do this about a week before the interview, you will have time to get used to your new haircut. Most people look best in their natural hair colour, and this is evident when they are wearing clothes to complement their natural colouring.

Make-up
If you wear make-up, make sure that the style and colour do not date you. This is another area where women often lack confidence, because they are bombarded with conflicting advice from advertisements and magazine articles, but do not seek specialist help. Again, one trip to an image consultant can solve these problems and you will be given advice on the best colours and style of make-up to suit you.

If the interview is important, it is worth taking the time and trouble to wash your hair and have a bath beforehand. Make sure that your hands are clean and your nails manicured.

There is also no point in wearing smart clothes if they are not clean. Shirts or blouses that have not been ironed are particularly noticeable and create a sloppy look, regardless of how attractive they are. Body odour or greasy hair are not ways to impress any employer.

Behaviour

There are many books in your local library which will tell you about the scientific study of body language and non-verbal communication. Basically, we are all animals and respond to each other on a simple level in this way. When we meet other animals we need to know that we are not under threat. That is why *smiling* at another human being is such a powerful signal.

When we smile at other people we reassure them that we are not going to attack them, and being smiled at by others is the way *we* receive reassurance that the person facing us is not an enemy. Communication between people is much more relaxed and straightforward when we know we are safe. Think about how difficult it is to make conversation with your dentist before you have treatment! So, to create a good impression, start off the interview on a positive note by entering the room and smiling at all the interviewers present. Even if you are too scared to smile again, you will have started the interview in a confident way.

At the end of the interview when you leave, make sure you thank the interviewer for the time and attention you have been afforded and smile again to leave on the same, positive note.

Eye contact

Looking straight into somebody's eyes when he or she is talking tells the person that you are interested, attending to what is being said and have nothing to hide. When we feel shy, it is sometimes awkward to keep this direct gaze on the interviewer. If you find this difficult, at least try to look at the interviewer when he or she is asking you a question, even if you look elsewhere during your response. If you are being interviewed by more than one person, do not always try to include all the panel in your glance. Instead, when one interviewer asks you an individual question, treat that person as though he or she is the only one interviewing you.

Posture

Other important aspects of body language for an interview are those relating to posture. We can all make ourselves invisible when we wish to and I am sure all women know how to do this. Imagine that you have missed the last bus and have to walk home alone in the dark. What do you do so as not to attract attention?

You hunch your shoulders slightly, look ahead or perhaps down at your feet, walk purposefully but not too fast, and definitely do not meet the eyes of anyone you pass. The look on your face is expressionless and you do not make any noise. You try to cover up as much of yourself as possible with your outer garments to disguise your gender. These tactics will probably work and enable you to look so anonymous that you will reach home untroubled by drunks or trouble-makers.

Now, bearing that example in mind, it should be easy to see how to create the opposite effect when you want to attract attention and be remembered. You must walk tall, pulling yourself up by the shoulders to increase your height and make your spine straight. You will look around you in an alert way and meet any other person's gaze directly, while smiling confidently at everyone you meet.

I hope this illustrates the control we all have over the way we are perceived by other people. In the interview, you do not want to appear insignificant or unremarkable. You want the interview panel to be left with a striking and positive impression of you physically.

When you sit down in the interview, make sure that your bottom is set well back on the seat, with your spine held fairly straight and supported by the back of the chair. Leaning forward slightly gives an impression of keenness. Do not slouch or sprawl in your seat – it implies that you are not taking the interview seriously. Practise in advance to find out which seating position is most comfortable for you. It does not matter whether your legs are crossed or not, but do not keep changing their position or you will distract the interviewer from what you are saying.

Gestures
Hands should be lightly clasped in your lap. Gestures add variety to speech, and your natural style may be to use your hands in this way occasionally. Too much gesticulation implies anxiety, so monitor this when you are practising your answers in front of the mirror.

Confidence

Confidence has been mentioned before as though it should be easy to acquire. Everybody is confident about their abilities in some activity or other. If I asked you to tell me something that you felt confident about, it could be cookery, playing sport or a hobby. If you analyse *why* you are confident at that particular activity, what would you attribute it to? Are you confident because it is a familiar task; because you have been told that you are good at it; because you are well prepared; or because you have studied how to do it?

Often, all these reasons apply, and that is why practising your interview technique is so valuable. Half the terror of an impending interview is because you do not know what to expect. Rehearsing in advance means that you will feel reasssured about which questions may come up, and about your ability to answer them.

Increase your confidence by packing carefully any items you might need if you are going to give a presentation, eg handouts or flip-chart pens.

The journey

The journey to the interview can be a source of anxiety. Plan in advance how much time to allow. If possible, do a 'dummy' or practice run and make sure that you can find the right building. Allow extra time for unforeseen hold-ups. It is important to be on time for your interview, so plan to arrive 15 minutes early. If you are delayed for any reason, telephone to let the company know and inform them of your expected time of arrival – although if you arrive too late you may miss the chance of being interviewed altogether. Remember that *everybody* you talk to at the company may be asked for their opinion of you – including the secretary or receptionist at the front door.

Voice

Interview nerves affect people in different ways. Some people speak very softly, some talk too fast and start gabbling, others become hesitant and leave long gaps between words. Some people stammer under pressure and some just answer briefly, replying 'yes' or 'no' whenever possible, rather than speaking up about themselves. None of these responses is helpful in an interview.

We have already noted that the whole purpose of your being invited along is for the interviewer to find out as much as possible about you in the time available. Short, quiet, babbled or hesitant answers will not suffice. Of course, any experienced interviewer will make allowances for initial nerves, but will expect you to settle down to the task in hand fairly quickly.

Just try to imagine that you are talking to someone you know fairly well, and speak in a relaxed and easy manner. Normally, the longer you worry about getting every word and phrase exactly right, the more tangled up you become. Pauses sound fine as part of ordinary speech and are preferable to 'ums' and 'ers'. Pauses only become a problem if they are excessively long, in which case an interviewer may not realise when you have finished speaking. If you know that you are prone to leaving such gaps in the conversation, you could mark the end of your answer by saying something like: 'Those are the main points that I want to make.'

Controlling nerves

Everybody suffers from nervousness in situations which create anxiety. Some of our greatest actors are literally sick before each and every performance, showing that the energy which is generated by nervous tension is crucial to giving a good performance. The trick is to make this tension work *for* you rather than against you.

When we are nervous the body reacts to the fact that the forthcoming event is important to us. We have spent time and trouble rehearsing for the interview and the body is getting its response mechanism ready either to fight or run away. This flight or fight mechanism is a throw-back to the times when we had to act in one of these ways to survive. We need to harness these nerves to make us fight, or at least act impressively before the interviewer, rather than panic and dry up.

In your life there will be many occasions which will bring on an attack of nerves, and knowing how to control it will come in useful. The main thing is to have some long-term goal to concentrate on and carry you through the experience. Like the actors who force themselves on stage because the show must go on, you can talk and impress people despite your nerves if you keep the purpose of the interview at the front of your mind all the time.

You have been invited to this interview so that the employer can find out about you, and you are going to tell the interviewer all about yourself. If you have prepared well for the interview, you will feel excited and enthusiastic about the idea of what you can contribute to the organisation.

This energy you have generated will carry you through the interview, and all the interviewer will remember about you will be your keenness and enthusiasm for the position rather than your nerves.

I once interviewed a series of people for a job requiring energy and commitment. Each one seemed competent and suitable, but none stood out. At the end of the last interview, the candidate said goodbye with the words: 'I would really love doing this job, you know.' Her obvious enthusiasm shone through her nervousness and I offered her the job on the spot, confident that she was the most suitable candidate. Showing enthusiasm does not mean being immature or sounding desperate to get a job. It requires a genuinely positive attitude to the challenges and opportunities that the vacancy offers.

Your nervousness does not show to other people as much as you think. I run workshops to prepare people for interviews where I make people do a mock interview in front of the whole group. Every single person admits to being terribly nervous, but the audience is always amazed that each interviewee seems calms and collected. Nerves just do not show. We may know that our palms are sweaty, our stomachs churning and our knees knocking, but no one else will realise our predicament.

When an attack of nerves strikes, the energy generated often escapes in repetitive gestures or mannerisms. Fidgeting with pens, twiddling strands of hair, constantly touching face or mouth are just some of the ways in which we show our nervousness and we are often unaware of such habits.

A good way to learn about nervous mannerisms is to ask yourself some of the practice questions which start on page 51, while watching your reflection in a mirror. This is your chance to see yourself as others see you. Alternatively, you could ask a friend or relative to give you some honest feedback on your behaviour under pressure. Hands are best kept under control, clasped lightly together in your lap.

The interviewer may also be experiencing some feelings of nervousness. Many managers have little experience or skill at conducting interviews. Moreover, in a panel interview there may be all sorts of tension between the representative from the personnel department, the line manager and the other members of the group of which you will not be aware.

Imagine that you have been asked to interview some job candidates. How would you feel? Perhaps a little apprehensive in advance and on the shaky side when the very first candidate comes into the room? You have never met this person before. Would you be totally confident about what to say and how to handle the candidates? Interviewing is a difficult task because it is stressful to be faced with someone whom we have to talk to in some depth but do not know.

It is comforting to know that most interviewers are nervous. An interview can be a disquieting experience for the people on both sides of the table. Obviously, the interviewer has a relatively more powerful position than the interviewee – he or she has a job to offer – but it is important to remember all the dynamics of the occasion.

Make sure that you visit the toilet before the interview and do not drink or take drugs to calm you down. Both will impair your performance, and alcohol can always be smelled on the breath.

Relaxation exercises

Breathing exercise

Breathing exercises are one way of managing feelings of nervousness. When we are under strain our breathing is likely to become shallow, and we do not use all our lung capacity. The effect is to starve the brain of the vital oxygen it needs in order to think quickly and clearly. Just before you enter the interview room, take several deep breaths.

This exercise is easiest to do when standing. Inhale slowly, breathing through your nose, and try to fill your lungs completely. After a count of three, slowly exhale through your mouth. Concentrate on expelling all the air that you took in. Feel your shoulders relax as you breathe out. Repeat this deep breathing four or five times.

You should see your stomach move out with each breath in, and flatten each time you breathe out. Do not take this exercise too far – hyperventilation is not necessary! The exercise should be carried out only in a gentle and rhythmic manner. If it is impossible to have some time on your own, with practice you should be able to breathe deeply without anyone noticing.

Facial exercise

Smiling has another benefit apart from putting the interviewer at ease. It is also an effective way of exercising your facial muscles. When we tense up, our faces can take on a stony expression and a frown of concentration. To relax your face, gently say all the vowel sounds a, e, i, o, u, and stretch your mouth in an exaggerated manner to make all your facial muscles flex. Repeat the exercise several times. Finish off with a big, wide grin. Make sure that you are not being watched while doing this exercise in case you frighten the other candidates!

To control your feelings of nervousness

1. Feel determined about what you want to say.

2. Keep in the forefront of your mind what you want to achieve.

3. Remember to do some deep breathing and to *smile*.

4. Remember that nerves never show as much as you think.

5. Bear in mind that the interviewer is probably under some strain too.

CHAPTER 5

Guidelines and examples

Examples of interview questions and answers

Here is a selection of typical questions that you may be asked in an interview. Following each question are some suggestions about the type of information that the interviewer would be interested in as part of your answer. You will rarely be asked *all* these questions, and some may not apply to you, but as full a range as possible has been included to give you practice at how to respond. If you can answer all these questions confidently you are truly ready for your interview.

You will see that a full answer for each question has been suggested. You are only being asked these questions to prompt you to talk about yourself. The more information you can give, the more helpful it will be, as long as your answers are concise, clear and relevant. Details are not as important as stressing what skills or experience you have gained.

Education and training

1. Why did you decide to go to college?
This requires a full answer, and you need to go back to when you left school in order to be able to answer it. What were your long-term ambitions at the time? Were there certain subjects you particularly enjoyed at school and wished to continue to study? How and why did you choose your particular course and your specialist subjects?

2. Can you tell me about your college course?

Many people forget to explain exactly where they went to college and precisely which course they took. Even if the employer already has this information on your CV or application form, he or she may not have it to hand, or even remember having seen it before. What sort of teaching methods were employed? Were there compulsory core subjects and specialist options? How did you decide which to study?

3. Did you enjoy any particular part of your studies more than the rest?

The employer is trying to find out what sort of person you are to get clues about the sort of work that would suit you best. Was there some particular option or course that you enjoyed more than others? Did it involve working alone or with other people?

Think about the impression you will create with particular answers. Talking at length about how much you enjoyed researching alone in the chemistry laboratory at college will indicate your preferred style of working. The interviewer will probably assume that you are not the team player that he or she is looking for.

4. Can you tell me about a project that you worked on at school or college?

Working life is full of dealing with projects of one kind or another, from getting a letter typed, to managing a building contract, to supervising a team of accounts clerks. This question is being asked because the answer will give an indication of the way you would deal with this kind of work. You will need to explain how the project was conceived, what the task was, who else was involved in the work, how you worked together, how you handled any difficulties, your particular contribution and what you think you gained from the exercise.

Employment history

5. Have you had any work experience?

This question is often asked of younger people who have just left full-time education. No employer wants to hear that you are completely inexperienced, even if you only left college a week ago. You will need to come up with some kind of answer in order to reassure the interviewer that you are used to the routine of work, that you can hold a position and that someone else has wanted to employ you in the past. Perhaps you have done a paper round; worked on voluntary projects while at school; had holiday or vacation jobs or participated in a work experience programme at school?

If you have never done any type of work at all, now is the time to start. You could offer your services to a community organisation on a voluntary basis or 'work shadow' some friend or relative who does what you are interested in. A training course could help you pick up many transferable skills. If you are studying it may be possible to get a Saturday or evening job. Apart from providing you with a positive response to this question, the work experience may gain you a character reference from the organisation concerned.

6. Can you tell me about your last job?
Again, it is not the precise details of what you were doing in the job that are wanted, but an account of the main skills involved and what you contributed to the organisation. Give concrete examples where possible to illustrate your points and stress how you have progressed in the course of the job.

7. Why did you leave your last position?
This is not the time to decry either your last job, the people you worked with or the employer concerned. A candidate who appears to have difficulty in getting on with people will definitely not be offered the position. Nobody wants to risk employing a trouble-maker. You will need to provide positive reasons for moving on from your last job, involving either different work or preferably taking up a new opportunity – to study, do voluntary work, or whatever you say you have been doing since you stopped work. If there were major problems in your last (or present) job that you wish to mention, you should only talk about possible improvements which could be made in order to sound positive.

If you are currently employed, make sure that you do not sound desperate to escape from your job. You must provide positive illustrations of the way you could contribute to the position for which you have applied.

8. What have you been doing since you left your last job?

This is a good question which you can easily use to your advantage. If you are not working, and even if you have been unemployed for some time, you must come up with something positive that you have been doing with your time since you last worked. It is not enough to say that you have been looking for another job – that will be assumed.

The best answer will be either that you have been doing some sort of course to improve your skills or that you have been doing some voluntary work. If you know someone who runs a business, it may be possible to say that you have been doing some freelance contract work, helping out with this company.

Whatever you say will need to be backed up with details of your activities, if the employer wishes to know more. If you are not doing anything with your time – you must start something immediately. Apart from being an absolute necessity for your CV and job applications, it is the perfect antidote to the depression that can come with unemployment.

9. What has been your greatest achievement in your working history?

Some hard thinking before the interview is needed in order to answer this question. The example that you choose should convey some of the principal qualities needed in the job applied for and should be explained clearly and concisely. A useful way to make sure you don't ramble is to structure your answer into three key points.

10. Can you tell me about a problem that you have had to deal with?

The point of this question, as far as the employer is concerned, is to see how you would tackle obstacles at work. An ideal answer would involve you in thinking through a difficulty and solving it with the help of other people. If you can indicate some general lessons that you learnt from the experience, so much the better.

11. What would you do if you had a problem that you could not deal with? Perhaps you are faced with a difficult customer.

Everybody has to ask for help at times during their working life. Your answer should show that you would not give up as soon as you were faced with a problem. The employer wants to see that you would be responsible and calm in your dealings with customers. Explain that you would try to find out the exact nature of the problem troubling the customer, while calming him or her down, if necessary. In many cases you would be able to sort out the problem yourself, but sometimes the issue needs to be dealt with at a higher level.

Tell the interviewer that you are aware that if this were the case you would need all the details in order to pass them on to whoever could sort out the problem. Apologising to the customer for the delay, you would tell him or her exactly when the problem would be attended to. You would then pass on the query to your supervisor or the person responsible.

12. Which of all your jobs have you found the most interesting, and why?

This question may be asked if you have had a varied employment history. A wise answer would include work similar to the job on offer to show that you will be happy and involved in your work. Try to justify your choice by giving examples of your main achievements in the time spent there, or explaining the particularly interesting aspects.

13. What are the most satisfying and the most frustrating aspects of your present/last job?

You may be asked this question to find out what you like best and least about your most recent position. Think carefully before you phrase your answer. The most satisfying aspects of the job should be those most closely linked to the position that you are now applying for. A long list of frustrations can make you sound like a moaner. If there was some particularly difficult aspect of the job, try to say how you helped to improve it.

Interests

14. What hobbies or interests do you have?
Why should employers be interested in the answer to this question? Is it pure nosiness? Everything you say about yourself contributes to the general impression gained about you. If I tell you that my hobbies are knitting, cookery, needlework, decorating cakes and bird-watching, you have an idea of the sort of person I am. If, however, I tell you that my hobbies include karate, African music, organising a community group, gardening and swimming, the picture is quite different.

You need to think hard about which hobbies and interests to mention. They can illustrate that you have a well-rounded personality and lead a full and satisfying life. Examples of times when you were in a leading or organising role will create a good impression.

There are some interests that we all have in common and these are not worth listing. We all read, watch television and socialise with other people, and these activities should not be part of your answer unless you have something specific to say about them. Be warned that if you mention them, you are likely to be asked either 'What was the last book you read?' or 'Can you tell me about a television programme that interested you lately?' Details of the latest episode of your favourite soap opera will not suffice!

Do not be too specific about any political or religious interests unless they are of direct relevance to the job in question. It is better just to say, as in the example above, that you are actively involved in the local community. The interviewer may hold different views from your own.

You do not have to spend time on all the hobbies that you mention, but be sure that you know enough to talk about the subject in some depth. Employers often pick on hobbies as an easy area of questioning and will be interested in discussing more unusual choices.

You should have some knowledge of every hobby that you mention, even if you need to say: 'Well, I am very interested in wind-surfing. At the moment I am finding out about it, but I intend to spend some time next summer having a go,' or 'I used to play a lot of basketball at school. I'm a bit rusty now, but I watch it when I can and am joining an evening class shortly to brush up my skills.'

The three points to be aware of when answering this question are:

- Include a variety of interests – some using your mind and some sporting or physical activities to show that you are a lively, healthy and active person.

- Ensure that you have at least one pastime which is different from other people's.

- Be prepared to discuss any of the topics you mention in some detail.

General

15. What are your strengths?

This is one of my favourite questions. If you were ever given a chance to shine – this is it. Although at first sight this seems daunting, it is easy to prepare an impressive answer if you consider it before the interview.

In the space below make a list of ten of your good qualities. Each point should compromise one word or short phrase and should relate to your behaviour at work.

Examples could be: 'Flexible; good at keeping to deadlines; calm; can work under pressure ...' Everybody's list will be different. If you find this exercise difficult, try to imagine what your mother, your best friend, your dog – or whoever loves you most in the world – would say about you if they were describing your best characteristics to a stranger.

YOUR TEN STRENGTHS

1. _____

2. _____

3. _____

4. _____

5. _____

6. _____

7. _____

8. _____

9. _____

10. _____

This list is very useful as the basis for answering any question about your strengths. By selecting five or six points from your list, you can put together a clear and powerful answer. Because you have prepared in advance, you will sound confident about your own abilities and proud of your character.

Most people find it hard to compile the list of their ten strengths, and even harder to talk about them in an interview. Do not worry about sounding boastful. It is much more common for candidates to be too modest than blow their own trumpets. I recommend that you don't hold back from explaining just how good you are in this answer.

The list of ten points can be kept and added to throughout your life. Whenever a colleague or friend compliments you on some aspect of your character, add it to your list. It will prove useful when you have to complete a CV, application form or go for interviews in the future, as well as providing a boost to your confidence when you need one!

16. What are your weaknesses?

Whatever does the employer mean by asking this question? Nobody will want to employ someone who can reel off a long list of serious faults. The best way to answer is not to admit to any weaknesses at all. If you do mention weaknesses, make sure that they are those which sound more like strengths. For instance: 'I sometimes take my work too seriously and will stay late at the office to get something finished', or 'I tend to be very flexible as a work colleague, and I will do the jobs that no one else wants to do'. No employer will mind you having weaknesses like these!

17. What are you most proud of?

This should normally relate to some work experience, and it is helpful if it can demonstrate the necessary qualities for the job on offer. Any project or team work where you played a significant role could be mentioned. Any instance where your contribution made a real difference, where you tried an innovative approach or learnt something new would be well worth mentioning.

18. Which current affairs problem have you been aware of lately?

This is a favourite question for public service jobs and is designed to check two things. The first is that your understanding of the world is wide and up to date, and the second is to see what sort of political attitudes you have. It therefore makes sense to read a quality daily newspaper thoroughly for at least a week before any interview. This is particularly relevant when you have applied for a job where you would be representing the views of the employing organisation.

Employers rarely want candidates to express strong political views in interviews. This is particularly true of the civil service, voluntary sector and local authorities. Ideally, you should illustrate that you know about a current issue in some depth, you are aware of the two sides to the argument, you can understand the feelings on both sides, and you realise what a difficult political problem it is.

Politics should be left to politicians, or to any of us in our private lives, not brought into the workplace. If you are asked for your opinion on a political issue, refrain from coming down heavily on either side. Government or local authority employers want to be sure that you are aware of the need to put into practice the wishes of the political masters of the day – and they can be right or left wing.

19. What do you see yourself doing in five years' time?

This is a similar question to one about your career ambitions. Think – why is the employer asking this? Does he or she want to know that you plan to train as an accountant or an actor in your spare time, and leave this job as soon as possible? No. He or she wants a member of staff who is serious about the vacancy and interested in staying put for a considerable time. Your answer could indicate that you hope to be in the company, but perhaps with greater responsibilities.

20. Why should we employ you rather than another candidate?

This is another good question as it enables you to use your list of ten strengths again. (See question 15 above.) Employers are interested in hearing about your skills, experience and personality.

In your answer you could mention any of your particular skills which relate to the job, your relevant experience, and add those aspects of your personality which best suit you for the position. A question like this is a gift to an interviewee. Do not be worried about boasting. This is the time to 'sell yourself' strongly to the interviewer. You are being asked to summarise your application – and the answer to this question is the crux of the whole interview.

You can bring in your ideas here – explain the thoughts you have had about the organisation and your vision for the future of the job.

21. What other careers are you interested in?

If you are applying for a computer operator's job in order to pay the rent and secretly want to be a police officer or a ballet dancer, keep that to yourself. Again, think – why is the employer interested in this question? He or she will be most impressed by the candidate who seems serious about the job on offer and about making a career in this line of work. Imply that your career ambitions are in this exact field. You could add that in the future you would be interested in working your way up to a position with more responsibility, or perhaps specialising in a particular area of the work.

22. Which other organisations have you applied to?

This question is similar to the one above. The employer does not want a candidate whom every other company has rejected. You want to convey the impression that you feel this particular vacancy is exactly the right one for you, and you have been saving yourself for it. I recommend that you say you are being choosy about the companies you approach. In other words, imply that you have not found such an interesting vacancy as this before.

23. What does equal opportunities mean to you?

This is the most difficult question to answer. But, fortunately, most interviewers are not too sure what the correct answer is. As long as you demonstrate that you understand the importance of everyone getting the same chances in employment and access to services, the employer will be impressed.

Many people answer: 'Treating everyone in the same way.' I think this answer is a little too simple. Some people with special needs may need extra help. You may have some personal awareness of this subject and feel like expressing it in the interview. For instance: 'As a woman, I know how it feels not to be taken seriously sometimes, so I always try to make sure that I treat everyone with respect,' or 'When I first arrived in this country I felt like an outsider and I am keen to help those who may need more support to make full use of the services offered by this organisation.'

24. How would you put equal opportunities into practice?
This is often asked together with the previous question. The trick is to think about the best answer in the light of the organisation applied to. Why has the employer decided to ask you this? It is likely that the current vacancy is with a large organisation, public company or local authority which is looking for staff who will be aware of two things: first, that services need to be made available to the whole population and, second, that colleagues may need support and understanding too. Explain how you would aim to fulfil these requirements in that job.

The vacancy

25. Tell me what you know about this organisation.
There is no excuse for not having a response to this question. Whatever the particular job that you are applying for, the interviewer will expect you to have some knowledge of the organisation, and the more the better. Whether you have seen an advertisement, been sent a job description or person specification, or read literature about the company, you should have some information to offer. The more you know, the more suitable you will seem.

If you have found no prior information then at least use your eyes and ears in the interview. Are there brochures or posters in evidence; how do the staff seem to relate to each other and outsiders, what first impressions have you gained? Sharing your thoughts on these topics, always stressing positive points, will show you are alert and interested.

26. Why do you want to work for this company?
Answering this question depends on the type of work offered and how much you know about the company concerned. You need to stress the particular type of organisation in relation to your own skills, strengths and personality. Your ideas about what you would do if offered the job are worth contributing here.

27. If you were offered this job, how do you think you would spend your first two weeks with the company?

This is a more general question designed to check that you have a realistic and sensible approach to work. In most jobs, unless you have worked for the organisation before, you need to spend your first few days getting used to the new environment. This means finding your way around, meeting your new colleagues, and familiarising yourself with the rules and working practices. You would also probably spend some time with your new manager learning how the work is done and about current priorities.

28. What do you think are the most important issues facing this organisation at the moment?

This question may well be posed when certain political or financial issues affect an organisation. Examples of such organisations could be charities, voluntary organisations or local authorities. Your answer would depend on the exact nature of the employer, but could include: generating income; allocating scarce resources; setting objectives; implementing cutbacks; quality control; managing grant-funding or some particular campaign with which the organisation is involved.

29. What do you think you can contribute to this company?

This is one of my favourite questions. As far as an employer is concerned, this represents the crux of the whole interview. This is your chance to shine, by saying exactly why you decided to apply for the job. You will need to bring out your particular strengths and show exactly what you can offer. Quoting your experience and skills will help to impress on the employer that you will be a valuable addition to the team. Don't forget to include good points about your personality here. Move on to explain how you would use all these things to help build on the success of the organisation.

30. Why are you applying for the post?

This is another variant on the last question and should be answered in the same way. Try to structure your answers.

Give three key points such as:

1. my skills and experience;

2. my character and personality;

3. my vision for this particular post.

In this way you will give a clearer response while still including everything you need to say.

Dos and dont's

Do   let go! The interviewer wants to get to know who you are, so feel free to be yourself.

Do   mind the gap! Make a positive statement about things that would otherwise look negative.

Do   speak up for yourself – you have nothing to lose and everything to gain. Think of the interview as a kind of performance, you need to be a bit 'larger than life'.

Do   take care with your appearance; consider every aspect of your presentation.

Do   keep your answers simple and clear.

Do   speak as you would normally; there is no need to put on an act by using long words or complicated sentences.

Do   boast about your strengths and achievements – all the other candidates will be trying to make themselves look extra good too.

Don't   lose your confidence; concentrate on the vacancy that you are interested in.

Don't   worry about nerves – they never show to other people as much as you think they do.

Don't   smoke or drink tea or coffee in the interview.

Don't assume that the interviewer knows what you are talking about – the things that you think are obvious may
be unclear to others.

Don't ever give just 'yes' or 'no' answers – the employer will
want to know more than that.

Don't use jargon or specialised terms without an explanation.

Don't lie about yourself – you could face dismissal if you
obtain a job under false pretences.

Dealing with tricky situations

Starting off the interview

I recommend shaking hands with the interviewer when you
enter the room; it shows that you are keen to meet him or her
and able to be formally polite. Women sometimes find this
difficult, as shaking hands has in the past been more of a male
habit. Do not worry if you feel that it would be beyond your
capabilities, in a nervous state, to walk in and confidently
grasp a stranger's hand, but do respond positively if the interviewer wants to greet you in this way.

You will normally be invited to sit down but, if the interviewer does not mention it, do not immediately assume that
he or she is playing some fiendish trick to see how you react
under pressure. The much more likely explanation is that he
or she has simply forgotten to invite you to be seated, in their
concern about which question to ask you first. The solution is
to smile and ask politely: 'May I sit down?'

Good manners

On the subject of politeness, you can never be too polite in
interviews. On leaving I recommend saying: 'Thank you very
much for your time. I have enjoyed meeting you. Goodbye.'
Even if you are a habitual smoker, resist the temptation at the
interview. Falling ash and smoke surrounding the interviewee never look impressive, even if the employer is smoking.

Some people feel that if they are offered tea or coffee, it is
impolite to refuse. But it is best *not* to accept. In my personal

experience, nervousness only leads to disasters such as the cup falling on the floor or the drink filling the saucer or splashing on your interview suit. Have a strong cup of coffee after the interview is safely over.

If you do not understand or hear a question properly, do not panic. Just ask the questioner to repeat the question. It is better to do this than guess at what was said and make a mistake.

Money
Most jobs give some indication of the salary or wages in the advertisement or job details. If money is not mentioned, avoid discussing the subject at the interview. You will obviously not take any job without knowing what you are going to be paid, but you can always check on this when the interview is over. If you are offered the job, you can say: 'I'm certainly interested in the position, but haven't yet had full details about the conditions of employment. Perhaps you could tell me the salary for the job?'

The interview does not go as planned
If you have planned your responses but do not have the chance to get your points across, you can sometimes hijack the interview so that it goes more in your favour. Suppose that you had not been asked about your strengths, and want to bring in some of the points from your list of ten characteristics. At the end of the interview you could say: 'I would just like to add a brief comment about the sort of person I am' and then say your piece.

Panic sets in
Even the most well-prepared candidate can suffer from temporary drying-up in mid-interview. If your mind goes blank, breathe deeply and play for time by saying something like: 'That's an interesting question.' This allows you a few extra seconds to collect your thoughts. If you are really stuck, ask if you could return to that question later in the interview.

Don't know the answer?

Occasionally, you may be faced with a question that is just too difficult. If you cannot think of anything to say on a subject, explain so simply and without being embarrassed. If possible, indicate that it is an area you are keen to explore. Afterwards, do not let it worry you, but move on to the next question, clear that you are doing the best you can.

CHAPTER 6

Bringing it all together

Step-by-step checklist

Step 1. Planning

In order to feel confident you need to plan how to convince the employer that you are the best candidate for the position. Be familiar with the job that you will be interviewed for. Collect any helpful information about the company. Go over your application for the post and carefully analyse the specific vacancy to see what the employer is looking for. The successful candidate will plan to bring out in the interview those examples of his or her background, skills and personality which complement the ones required for the position. Think about the possible challenges and opportunities of the past to give you a picture of what you would do once offered the position.

The most important point to convey is that you are the right type of person for the job. Study your list of ten character strengths (see page 58). Select which will be the most useful at the interview. Construct sentences using the points that you have chosen, giving examples of the relevant type of behaviour. The details of previous experiences are not as important as your main achievements, the transferable skills learned or the way in which you behaved.

Mind the gap! Gaps can be literally breaks in your employment history or events that you need to convey in a positive light. You need to ensure that you do not sound apologetic about your experiences but can illustrate what you have learned from them. The most important thing about your answers is that they should all be positive – about your previous experience, your skills and strengths, and what makes you right for this particular job.

You can plan your journey in advance; allow extra time to ensure that you arrive at least 15 minutes early for your appointment. There is also some planning work to be done on your physical presentation. Decide which clothes to wear, concentrating on the most flattering style and colours for you. Take professional advice if necessary – a visit to an image consultant can be great fun.

Step 2. Preparation

You need to prepare yourself thoroughly for the interview. Do a dummy run of the journey to the organisation concerned if it is in an unfamiliar area. A vital part of your preparation concerns the clothes you will wear. They should all be clean, well ironed and look immaculate. Have a bath and wash your hair before the interview. Give due consideration to your accessories which can contribute to the employer's important first impression of you.

The most vital aspect of the preparatory stage is to speak aloud the answers that you have planned. This rehearses you for the actual performance and increases your confidence when you are asked the questions for real. Think what the interviewer is going to want to hear from you. You must sound keen and interested in the job; be someone with the right skills or be trainable, and show that you can fit into the organisation.

When you are practising your answers with a friend or in front of the mirror, be aware of how you look and sound. Your voice should be steady and clear. Try to smile while you are talking and see how it improves the way you look. Rehearse your walk; holding yourself up straight can reinforce the impression of confidence as well as making it easier to breathe.

Step 3. Generating confidence

This is the time to let your enthusiasm show. One of the most attractive attributes in a job candidate is a genuine interest in the work. Do not worry about your nerves – just concentrate on enjoying the interview. You are well prepared and confident that you are the right candidate for the job, and you can look forward to meeting the employer and telling him or her about yourself.

Before the event itself, relax your face with the exercise on page 49 and take some deep breaths (see page 48). Walk in with your head held up and a broad smile to make everyone present feel more at ease. The interviewer is probably quite nervous too. Shake hands if you can and remember to thank the interviewer for his or her time when you leave.

Make sure that you speak loudly and fully enough to do justice to your skills and strengths. The employer genuinely wishes to hear what you have to say so do not hold back from talking about yourself and your achievements.

Step 4. Follow-up

It is wise to apply for more than one vacancy at a time, so you always have more interviews ahead of you. This helps to keep a sense of perspective about the process and keeps you from feeling demoralised if you don't get a job. It is easy to become depressed about lack of success in job interviews. However, the most expert interviewees may be turned down just because, on the day, there happened to be somebody who seemed more suitable.

If you are rejected, it is worth contacting the employer to ask for some feedback on your performance in the interview. Most employers are keen to help as long as the request is phrased politely. I suggest something like:

'I have just attended an interview with you. Although I was not successful, I wondered if I could ask you for any feedback on my performance in the interview, as I am particularly interested in this type of work and your comments might help me in the future.'

Another antidote to feeling despondent about searching for work is to mix with other people in the same situation. A supportive group can keep you going when you feel at the end of your tether. At times you will need to fight the feeling that there is something wrong with you as a person. Sharing your experiences with other people will remind you that there are other excellent candidates who fail to get jobs. Maintaining some semblance of a work routine is also helpful in keeping up morale. Voluntary work, for example, provides contacts, experience, and a sense of purpose and self-worth.

If you keep getting invited to interviews then you know that your written applications are of a high standard. If you keep attending interviews, always doing your best and trying to improve, you will eventually get a job. Strongly resist feeling demoralised, depressed or unconfident. It was said earlier that interviews should be treated as learning experiences. Even if you are not successful at an interview, you can feel comfortable in the knowledge that you have done your best to create a good impression. Imagine that I am a fly on the wall, urging you on to speak up, let your personality out and enjoy the experience. Good luck!

Other sources of help

The Careers Service
In some areas of the country, the staff in your local careers service can offer help and advice to adults. They will have reference books about employers and applying for jobs as well as understanding and skilled staff who can help you put your CV together if you get stuck. They may also help you plan and rehearse for an important interview, or refer you somewhere which can. Find the phone number in the local phone book and ring them to find out more.

Employment Agencies
Agencies may help you prepare for a meeting with an employer for a particular type of job. They charge the employer if you are placed with a company.

Private Careers Counsellors
You can get help from careers counsellors who work privately and will make a charge for their service. This can be very

expensive although they will help coach you for different interview situations.

Learning Direct

The Learning Direct number, 0800 100 900, is a Government funded telephone helpline available to everyone. Ring the freephone number and you will be given advice about local sources of help on careers and learning issues. This could include where to contact the types of organisations mentioned above.

Further reading from Kogan Page

From CV to Shortlist: Job hunting for professionals, Tony Vickers, 1997

Get the Job You Want in 30 Days, Gary Joseph Grappo, 1998

Great Answers to Tough Interview Questions, Martin John Yate, 4th edition, 1998

How to Master Psychometric Tests, Mark Parkinson, 1997

How to Master Personality Questionnaires, Mark Parkinson, 1997

How to Pass Selection Tests, Mike Bryant and Sanjay Modha, 2nd edition, 1998

How You Can Get That Job! Application forms and letters made easy, Rebecca Corfield, 2nd edition, 1999

I Hate Giving Presentations, Michael D Owen, 1998

Marketing Yourself and Your Career, Jane Ballback and Jan Slater, 1998

Net that Job! Using the World Wide Web to develop your career and find work, Irene Krechowiecka, 1998

Powerful Presentations, Jöns Ehrenborg and John Mattock, 2nd edition, 1997

Preparing Your Own CV, Rebecca Corfield, 2nd edition, 1999

Readymade CVs, Lynn Williams, 1996

Readymade Interview Questions, Malcolm Peel, 2nd edition, 1996

Readymade Job Search Letters, Lynn Williams, 1995

30 Minutes Before Your Job Interview, June Lines, 1997

30 Minutes to Prepare a Job Application, June Lines, 1997

Index

Index